My Little Heavenly Helper

Hidden Pictures and Mazes

BRIGHTER CHILD®

Columbus, Ohio

Send all inquiries to:
School Specialty Publishing
8720 Orion Place
Columbus, OH 43240-2111

ISBN 0-7696-3250-5

2 3 4 5 6 7 8 9 10 MAZ 11 10 09 08 07 06

Table of Contents

Old Testament Hidden Pictures. 5–32

Learning the Books of the Bible. 33

All Through the Bible Mazes. 34–62

Hidden Pictures Answer Key. 63–64

Noah Walks With God

Noah loved God. When God told Noah to build an ark, he obeyed.

Find and circle these hidden objects: saw, sailboat, thermos, needle, bird, lamp, candle, hand mirror, and mouse.

Abraham Obeys

God told Abraham to leave his country and his people and go to a faraway land, where God would bless him.

Find and circle these hidden objects: sock, toothbrush, baseball, apple, glass, cap, feather, briefcase, and ice-cream cone.

Sarah Laughs

Three visitors came to see Abraham and Sarah. One visitor, the Lord, promised that Sarah would have a child. Sarah laughed.

Find and circle these hidden objects: sailboat, football, banana, two fish, door, mitten, ruler, and question mark.

A Ram for Abraham

Sometime after Isaac was born, God tested Abraham. God told Abraham to sacrifice his son. Abraham trusted that God would provide.

Find and circle these hidden objects: loaf of bread, pencil, goblet, match, broom, bird, candle, log, hockey stick, and fish.

Jacob's Dream

Jacob was on his way to find a wife. He stopped to sleep. He dreamed about a stairway that reached up to heaven.

Find and circle these hidden objects: teapot, two fish, banana, fan, apple, flashlight, and muffin.

Joseph's Dream

Joseph had a dream. In Joseph's dream, his brothers' bundles of grain bowed down to his grain.

Find and circle these hidden objects: bird, three fish, hand mirror, golf club, apple, heart, dog bowl, and sailboat.

Joseph in Charge

Pharaoh had two bad dreams. Joseph was able to tell him what they meant, so Pharaoh put Joseph in charge of Egypt.

Find and circle these hidden objects: flashlight, ax, flowerpot, horseshoe, broom, dolphin, bread, and goblet.

Baby in a Basket

Moses' mother, Jochebed, put her baby son in a basket and set it in the Nile River. His sister, Miriam, kept watch.

Find and circle these hidden objects: lemon, three fish, bread, donut, worm, ram's horn, bottle, and paintbrush.

Moses and the Red Sea

Moses lead the Israelites through the Red Sea on dry ground.

Find and circle these hidden objects: boat, oar, bird, beach ball, spoon, eyeglasses, kayak, and wedding ring.

Rahab and the Spies

Rahab hid the Israelite spies. She was spared when Jericho fell.

Find and circle these hidden objects: book, ladder, broom, glass, pizza slice, candle, hat, swan, and eyeglasses.

Joshua and the Battle of Jericho

With shouts and trumpets, Joshua led the Israelites to victory.

Find and circle these hidden objects: boot, pipe, CD, slice of bread, squirrel, thermos, book, ladder, cup, dinosaur, and teapot.

Deborah the Judge

Deborah was Israel's only female judge. She went with Barak, the commander, and his army when they fought and defeated the Canaanites.

Find and circle these hidden objects: ram's horn, harp, heart, apple, vase, rabbit, bird, and gavel.

Gideon Defeats the Midianites

With God's help, the judge Gideon defeated a vast army with only a few men and no weapons.

Find and circle these hidden objects: flashlight, lamp, glass, mouse, eagle, lightbulb, ram's head, crown, fish, chocolate chip cookie, and goblet.

Samson Pulls Down the Walls

God blessed Samson with amazing strength. He used it to destroy the evil Philistines.

Find and circle these hidden objects: comb, brush, dumbbell, lion's head, fox, dolphin, paper clip, ice-cream cone, bee, and boot.

Ruth and Naomi

Ruth left her country and provided for her mother-in-law in a strange land. Because of this, Boaz married her.

Find and circle these hidden objects: banana, helmet, birthday cake, sock, ear of corn, sailboat, bread, and rabbit's head.

Hannah's Prayer

Year after year, Hannah prayed for a son. God heard her prayers.

Find and circle these hidden objects: candle, praying hands, match, boot, musical note, snail, mouse, book, fish, pencil, and snake.

Samuel Hears God

Samuel went to live in the temple when he was very young. One night, God called Samuel. Samuel grew up to be a priest, prophet, and judge.

Find and circle these hidden objects: butterfly, ring, plunger, bugle, paper clip, two birds, flute, and sailboat.

David and Goliath

When David was just a boy, he defeated the mighty giant, Goliath, with only a slingshot and a stone.

Find and circle these hidden objects: bone, bear, CD, sheep, egg, bird, brush, hoe, fox, crayon, and glass.

Abigail the Brave

Abigail gave food to David and his men and kept David from murder.

Find and circle these hidden objects: bowl, pizza, popsicle, bird, snake, mushroom, flower, fork, spoon, and flashlight.

Wise King Solomon

Two women came to Solomon. One claimed that the other woman had stolen her baby. Solomon made a wise decision.

Find and circle these hidden objects: crown, flower, cup, brush, bird, lion, bread, heart, spear, fork, watch, arrow, and slippers.

Elijah and the Widow

During a famine, Elijah stayed with a widow and her son. God kept the woman's jar of flour and jug of oil full until rain fell.

Find and circle these hidden objects: loaf of bread, spoon, mouse, bear's head, heart, carrot, dolphin, and bird.

Elijah Is Lifted Up to Heaven

As Elisha watched, Elijah was taken up to heaven in a whirlwind, riding on a chariot of fire.

Find and circle these hidden objects: bird, mouse, bull, two candles, shark, banana, teapot, maple leaf, and heart.

Elisha Feeds a Crowd

Elisha fed a crowd of 100 people with just twenty small barley loaves.
God multiplied the loaves and food was left over.

Find and circle these hidden objects: banana, spoon, wolf, flashlight, ice-cream
cone, paintbrush, plate, jug, and bird.

King Josiah

Josiah was eight when he became king. During his reign, the Book of the Law was found, idols were destroyed, and the Passover was celebrated.

Find and circle these hidden objects: sailboat, bird, candle, snail, fish, lamp, needle, and lightbulb.

Queen Esther

Queen Esther risked her life to save her people, the Jews.

Find and circle these hidden objects: pot, broom, pencil, football, hoe, brush, lion's face, porcupine, and fan.

Three Men in a Fiery Furnace

Shadrach, Meshach, and Abednego were thrown into a fiery furnace because they would not bow down to a statue. God protected them.

Find and circle these hidden objects: envelope, ice-cream cone, bird, shark, candle, heart, spoon, and glass.

Daniel Prays

Daniel was wise and was faithful to God. He was thrown into a lions' den because he prayed to God. An angel kept Daniel safe.

Find and circle these hidden objects: loaf of bread, bird, sailboat, rabbit, spoon, mouse, scissors, swan, lemon, and paintbrush.

Jonah Tries to Flee

God called Jonah to preach against the Ninevites. Jonah tried to run away by taking a ship to Tarshish. After three days inside a whale, he obeyed.

Find and circle these hidden objects: fish, vase, spoon, bird, fork, heart, umbrella, and candle.

The Bible: The Book of All Books

The Bible is the book of all books. It is the special book that tells of God's amazing plan to save us so that we can live with God in His kingdom. The Bible is also a library of books. Under one cover, there are 66 separate books.

Color the path that shows all 66 books in order. You can go down, to the right, or to the left.

In the Beginning

Genesis, which means "beginning," is the first book of the Bible. The stories of the creation and of the first people are found in this book.

God took six days to create the world and all that is in it. On the seventh day, God rested. Follow the maze to discover God's creations.

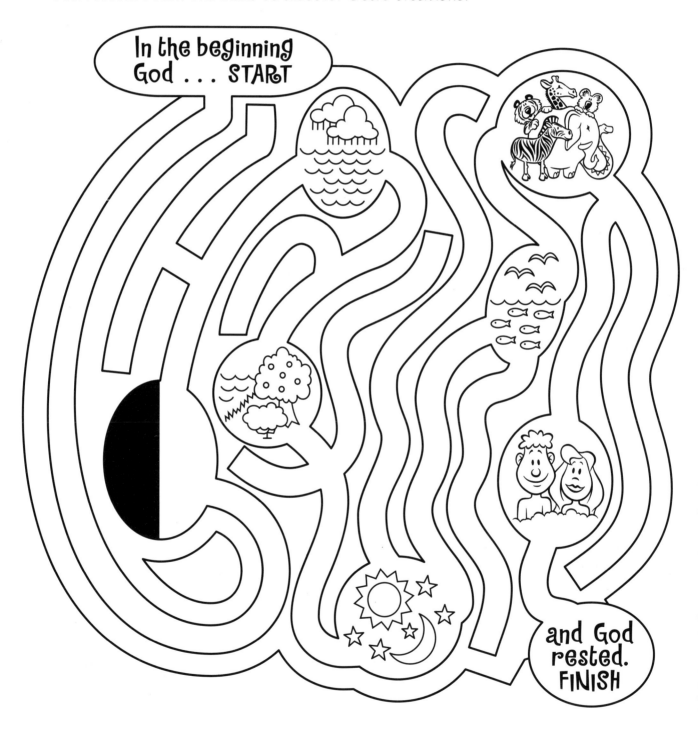

The Exodus: God Frees His People

Exodus tells the story of the exodus, one of the most important events in Old Testament history. It is the story of the Israelites' escape from slavery and their journey toward the Promised Land.

Moses was the Israelites' leader. Help Moses lead the Israelites to safety.

The Ten Commandments

The first five books of the Bible are called the books of the law. They contain God's rules for living. On Mount Sinai, God gave Moses the Ten Commandments, which were carved on two large stones. The first four commandments tell us how to love God. The next six tell us how to love others.

Find the path through the Ten Commandments.

The Books of History

The twelve books of history record God's work in the lives of the Israelites, the people of God. These books show how God cared for and guided these descendants of Abraham and Sarah.

Follow the path to find all the books of history in order.

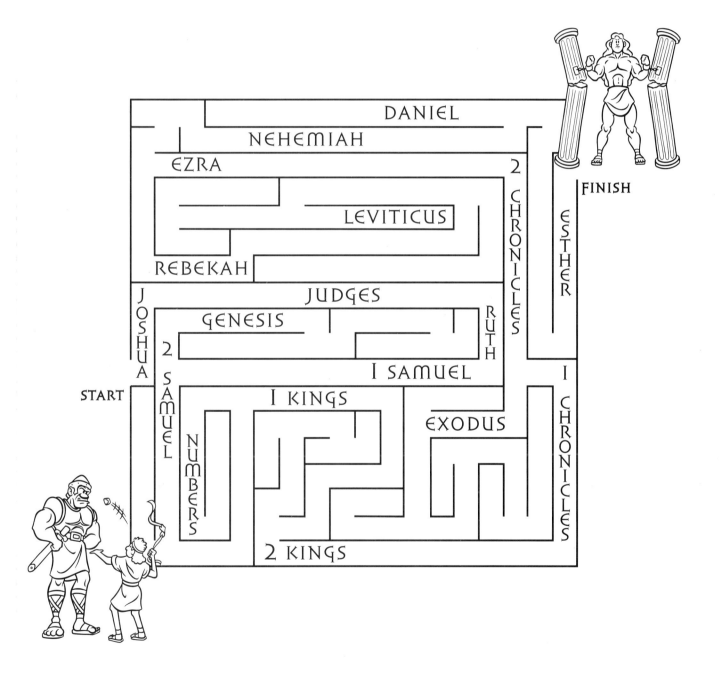

The Promised Land

After escaping Egypt, the Israelites wandered in the wilderness for 40 years. Finally, with Joshua as their leader, the Israelites were allowed to enter the Promised Land.

Follow the path to the Promised Land.

The Time of the Judges

When the people of Israel first settled in the Promised Land, they worshiped and served the Lord. But after Joshua died, many people began worshiping false gods. God raised up local judges to help the people remember the Lord. These judges included Deborah, Samson, and Gideon.

The pictures below are from the story of Gideon. Find the path through the torch. Then read Gideon's story in Judges 6–7.

Ruth and Naomi

The Book of Ruth is the story of Naomi's family. This book tells of Ruth and Naomi's return to Bethlehem and of Ruth's marriage to Boaz. Ruth became the great-grandmother of King David.

Help Naomi and Ruth find their way to Bethlehem.

A King for Israel

The people of God wanted a king. God had always told them that they were special: He was their king. But they insisted on having a human king. God finally allowed it. Saul was the first king chosen. Many kings came after Saul, but most of them did evil and led the people away from God.

Follow the trail of crowns to get to King Saul.

In Exile

The Israelites had trouble remembering the Lord. Even though God led them safely out of Egypt, brought their children to the Promised Land, and provided a king for them, they began to serve false gods. God punished them by allowing other nations to take them away from their homes.

Follow the path that leads the Israelites far from home.

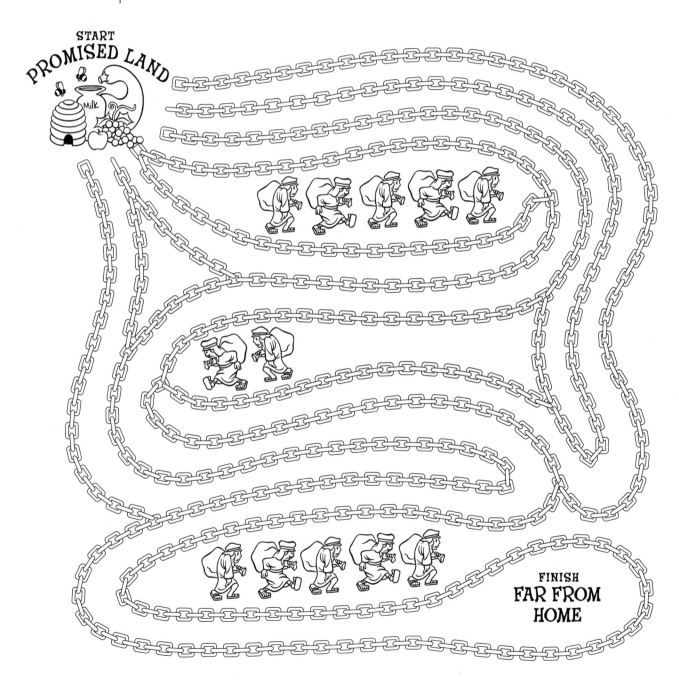

Queen Esther

In the Book of Esther, Queen Esther saved the exiled Jews in Persia from Haman, a wicked official of the king. Haman also made a gallows on which to hang Esther's cousin Mordecai. Esther exposed Haman's plan, and the king used the gallows to hang Haman.

Wind in and out and over and under to follow the paths of Esther and Haman.

The Books of Wisdom and Poetry

Some of the most beautiful and familiar words ever written are found in the wisdom and poetry books of the Bible: Job, Psalms, Proverbs, Ecclesiastes, and Song of Solomon.

Carefully stay on the path to find wisdom.

David and the Psalms

David was a giant-slayer, a king, a musician, and a writer. When he was a young boy, he was also a shepherd. David wrote many of the songs and poems that we find in the Book of Psalms.

Follow the path through the sheep to the calm, cool water.

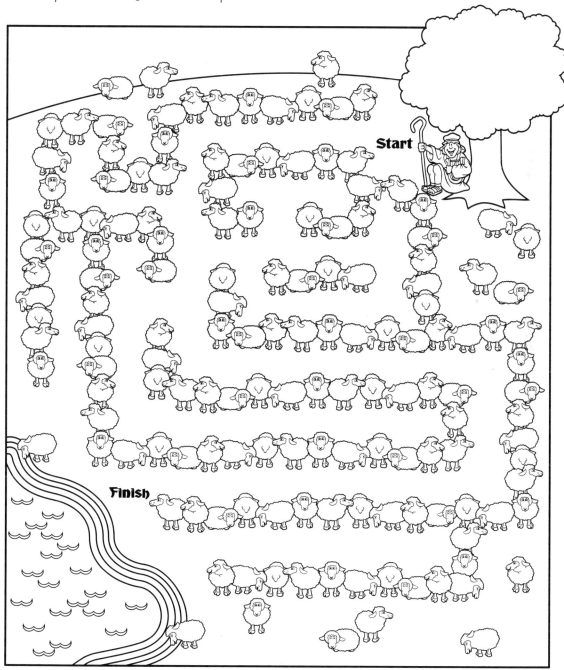

Solomon and the Proverbs

God told Solomon, "Ask for whatever you want." Solomon asked for wisdom. God gave him wisdom, plus other gifts such as riches and honor. Solomon wrote most of the wisdom books in the Bible. The Proverbs are short sayings that help people to stay on the wise path of life.

Solomon compared a wise person to an ant. Follow the ant to its nest.

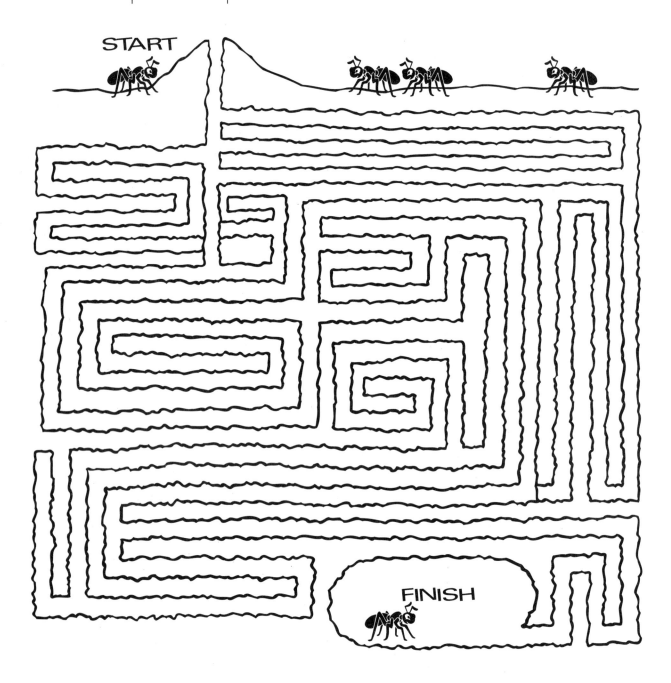

The Books of Prophecy

There are 17 books in the Old Testament called books of prophecy. The prophets were special people called by God. The prophets reminded the people to love God, and they foretold the future.

Follow the maze to find all 17 books of the prophets.

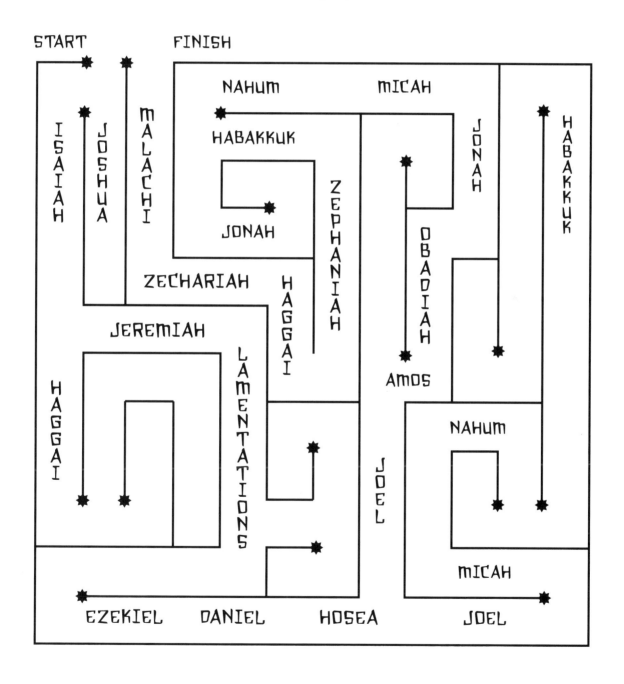

Isaiah, the Prophet

Isaiah's prophecy tells us wonderful words about Jesus, the Savior. The words below (found in Isaiah 9:6) were written hundreds of years before Jesus was born.

Follow the path to finish the verse.

For to us a child is born . . .
And he will be called . . .

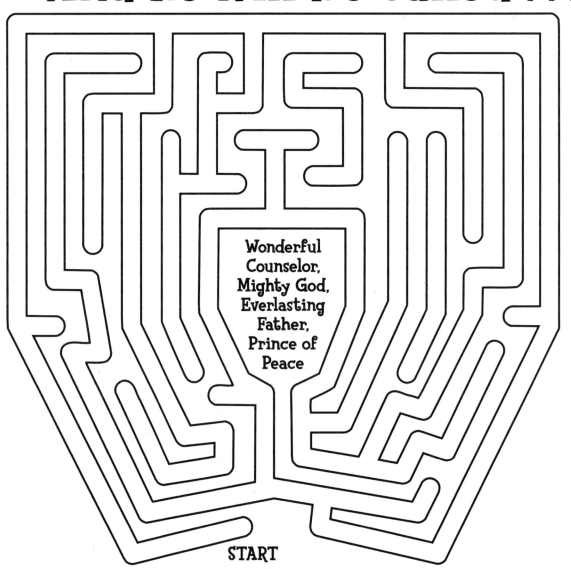

Wonderful Counselor, Mighty God, Everlasting Father, Prince of Peace

START

Jonah, the Reluctant Prophet

Jonah was a prophet who did not want to be a prophet. God told him to go to Nineveh to bring God's news. Instead of obeying, Jonah got on a boat headed for Tarshish. God sent a big fish to swallow him. Jonah spent three days in the fish's belly. When God again called him, Jonah obeyed.

Trace the way to Nineveh.

The New Testament Gospels

The New Testament begins with the four Gospels: Matthew, Mark, Luke, and John. The word *gospel* means "good news." The Gospels are full of good news about Jesus Christ.

Follow the four Gospel paths to learn something about each writer.

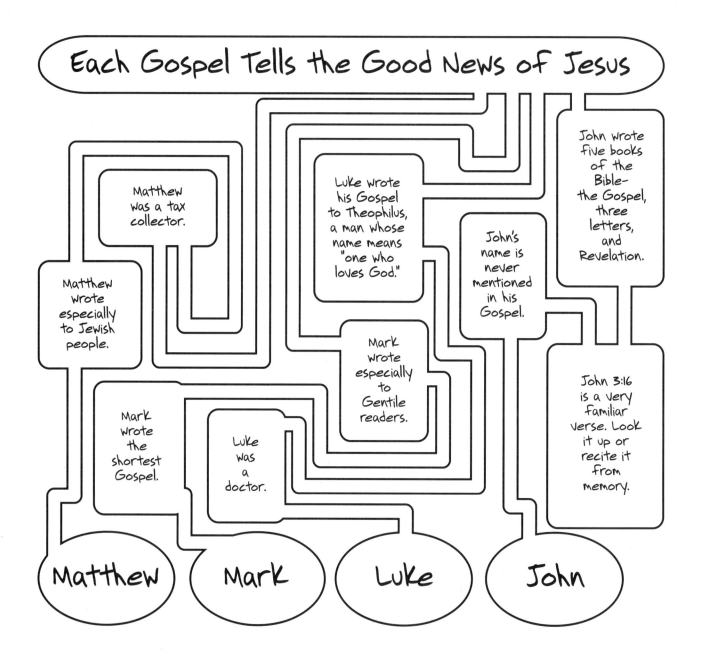

Each Gospel Tells the Good News of Jesus

Matthew was a tax collector.

Luke wrote his Gospel to Theophilus, a man whose name means "one who loves God."

John wrote five books of the Bible—the Gospel, three letters, and Revelation.

Matthew wrote especially to Jewish people.

John's name is never mentioned in his Gospel.

Mark wrote especially to Gentile readers.

Mark wrote the shortest Gospel.

Luke was a doctor.

John 3:16 is a very familiar verse. Look it up or recite it from memory.

Matthew   Mark   Luke   John

The Birth of Jesus

The good news for all people is that God came to earth as a baby, Jesus.

Journey through the path to Christmas.

Luke 1:26-38

Luke 2:13-14

Matthew 2:1-2

Matthew 1:18-25

Luke 2:8-12

Luke 2:6-7

Matthew 1:23

"God with us"

Luke 2:1-5

Merry Christmas
FINISH

START

Jesus Taught in Parables

Everywhere Jesus went, people gathered to hear him speak. He often spoke in parables, stories about everyday objects, persons, or situations that teach a lesson. Jesus told parables about such things as birds, fruit, coins, and camels. You can find the parables in the Gospels.

Jesus told a parable about a farmer who planted seeds. Some of the seeds did not fall in good soil. Help the farmer find the good soil.

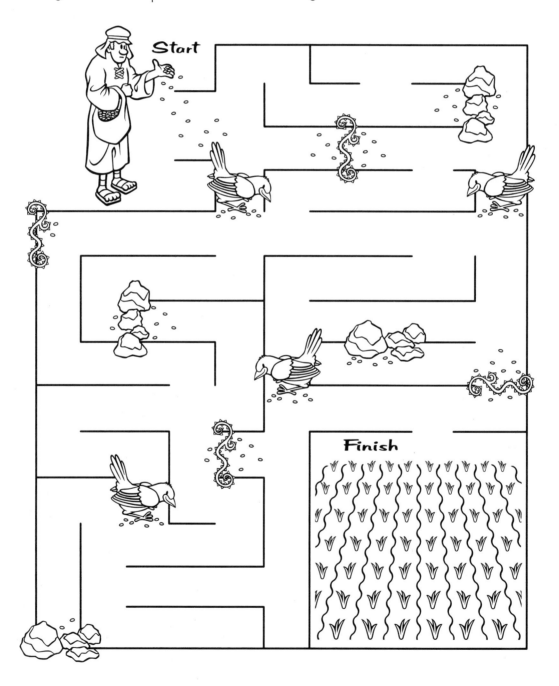

The Beatitudes

Jesus also taught through sermons. Perhaps the best known, the Sermon on the Mount, contains the beatitudes. The beatitudes teach spiritual values.

Follow the path through the "blesseds."

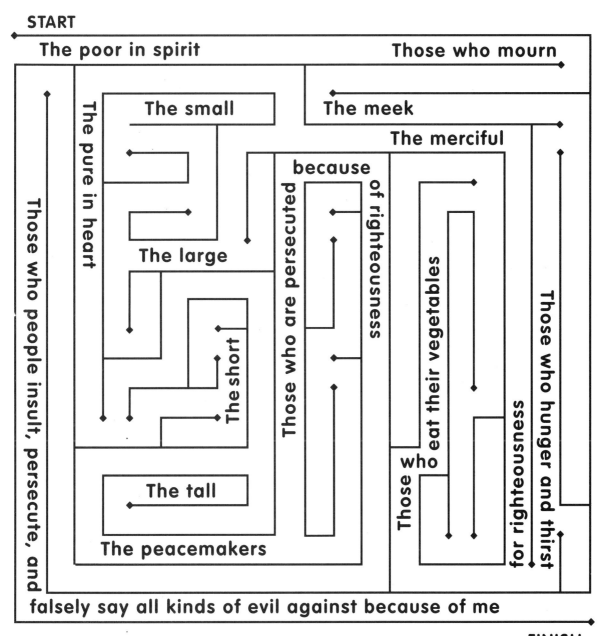

START

The poor in spirit

Those who mourn

The small

The meek

The pure in heart

The merciful

because

of righteousness

The large

Those who are persecuted

Those who eat their vegetables

Those who people insult, persecute, and

The short

Those who hunger and thirst

for righteousness

Those who

The tall

The peacemakers

falsely say all kinds of evil against because of me

FINISH

The Miracles of Jesus

Walking on water is just one of Jesus' miracles. The Gospels are full of the miracles of Jesus—people he healed, people he raised from the dead, crowds he fed, storms he stopped, and lives he changed forever.

Follow the path through the waves to help Jesus reach the boat of frightened disciples.

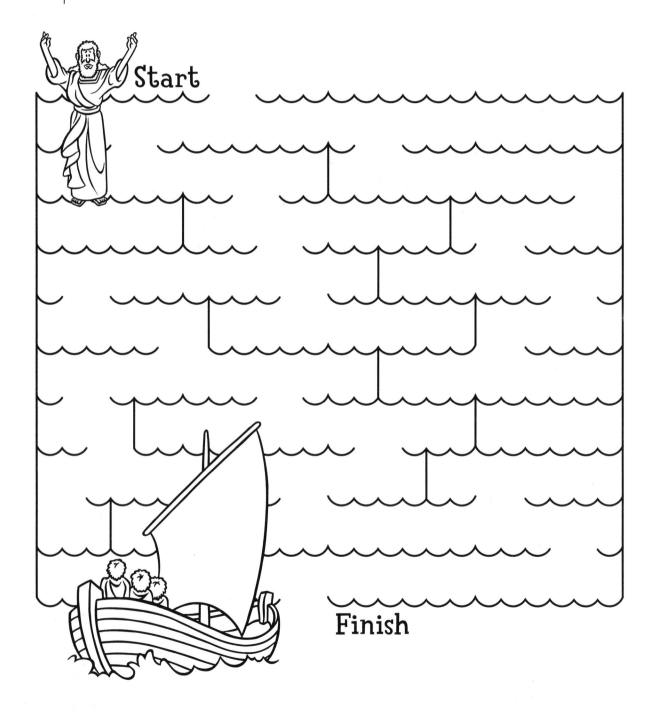

Start

Finish

Jesus Died for Everyone

The people of God in the Old Testament tried to love and serve God but often failed. Since before time, God had a special plan. When the time was right, Jesus came to earth to make things right between God and people everywhere. Jesus did this by dying on a cross. Read John 3:16.

Follow the maze to reach John 3:16 from all directions.

Jesus Is Alive!

Jesus conquered death. On the first Easter morning, Jesus' followers went to the tomb and found it empty! Jesus was not there. He was alive, and he lives today.

Help Jesus' followers find their way to the empty tomb.

START

FINISH

Jesus Returns to Heaven

After rising from the dead, Jesus spent some time with his followers. Then, telling the disciples to wait in Jerusalem for the promised Holy Spirit, he was taken up into heaven.

Follow the path through the clouds.

57

The Holy Spirit Comes to the Church

On the day of Pentecost, the disciples were filled with the Holy Spirit. Peter began to speak to the crowd. He told them all about Jesus. More than 3,000 people accepted the message and were baptized. The Book of Acts tells this story and the stories of many other acts of the apostles.

Help Peter follow the path to the growing church.

The Church Spreads

Paul and other Christians traveled around the known world starting churches and making disciples. The Book of Acts tells about how the church spread.

Follow the maze of letters to read what the Bible says about how the early church grew. Write the letters on the lines below.

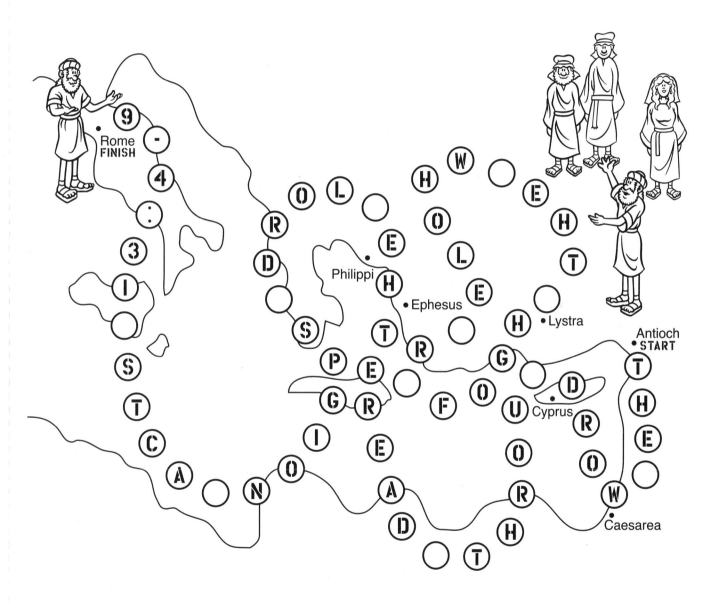

_____

_____

The Letters

Most of the New Testament books are letters written to early church members to help them grow closer to God and to serve Him. Today, Christians all over the world read the letters to learn the same things.

Follow the letter maze to its closing.

START

Dear friends, Let us love one another, for love comes from God. The Lord be with your spirit. Grace and peace be with you. In Christ, Jesus' servant

FINISH

Adapted from the letters 1 John & 2 Timothy

The Fruit of the Spirit

In Paul's letter to the Christians in Galatia, he reminds Christians that we belong to Jesus Christ and are to live by the Spirit. The Holy Spirit grows good fruit in our lives such as love, joy, and peace.

Find your way through the bowl of fruit. Circle the nine fruit of the Spirit.

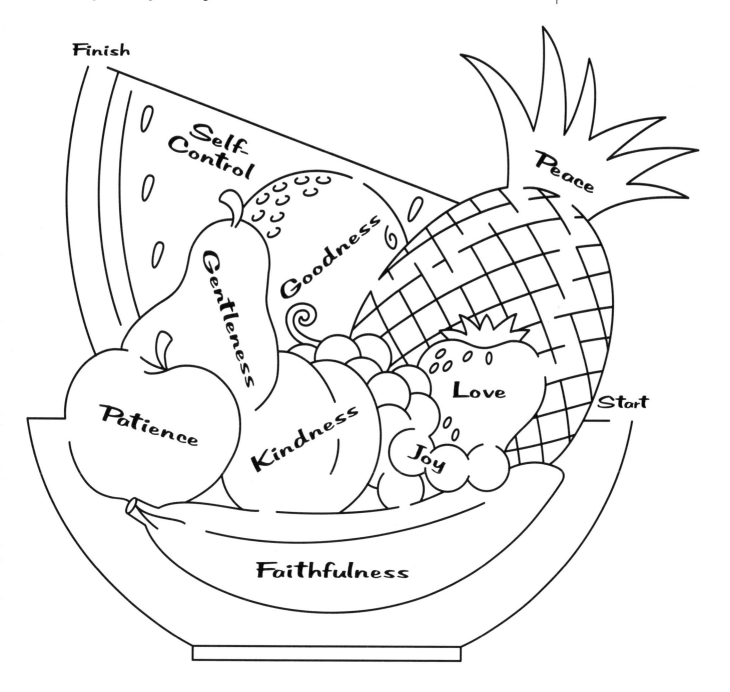

The End: The Book of Revelation

The last book in the Bible is called Revelation. It was written by John during a time when people in the church were being tortured for believing in Jesus. The Book of Revelation reminds us that Jesus is coming again and will create a new heaven and a new earth.

Can you find the path from earth to heaven?*

I AM COMING

FINISH A

A

START

B

B

* Fold the paper to match dots A to A and B to B to solve this mysterious maze.

Hidden Pictures Answer Key

Noah Walks With God—Page 5

Abraham Obeys—Page 6

Sarah Laughs—Page 7

A Ram for Abraham—Page 8

Jacob's Dream—Page 9

Joseph's Dream—Page 10

Joseph in Charge—Page 11

Baby in a Basket—Page 12

Moses and the Red Sea—Page 13

Rahab and the Spies—Page 14

Joshua and the Battle of Jericho—Page 15

Deborah the Judge—Page 16

Gideon Defeats the Midianites—Page 17

Samson Pulls Down the Walls—Page 18

Ruth and Naomi—Page 19

Hannah's Prayer—Page 20

Hidden Pictures Answer Key

Samuel Hears God—21

David and Goliath—Page 22

Abigail the Brave—Page 23

Wise King Solomon—Page 24

Elijah and the Widow—Page 25

Elijah Is Lifted Up to Heaven—Page 26

Elisha Feeds a Crowd—Page 27

King Josiah—Page 28

Queen Esther—Page 29

Three Men in a Fiery Furnace—Page 30

Daniel Prays—Page 31

Jonah Tries to Flee—Page 32